Contents

Let's Take a Trip Through Earth!

You might think Earth is all about green fields, rows of houses, or skyscrapers. This trip is going to change your mind! We are going on a journey of exploration into the center of Earth.

CH

Fantasy
Science
Field Trips

A Journey to the
Center
of the Earth

Claire Throp

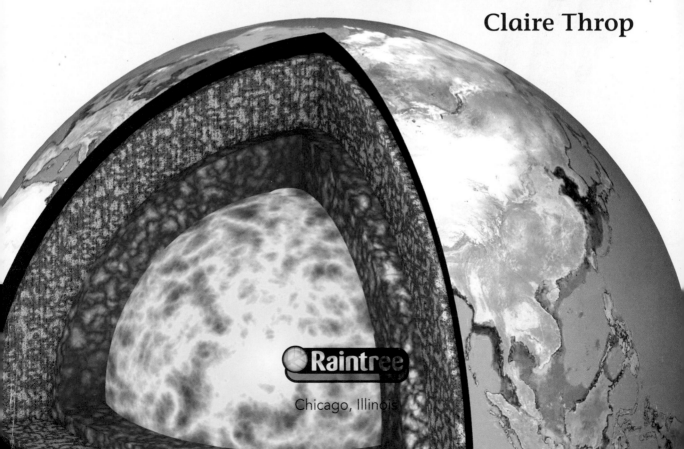

Raintree

Chicago, Illinois

Edited by Dan Nunn and Catherine Veitch
Designed by Cynthia Akiyoshi
Picture research by Ruth Blair
Production by Vicki Fitzgerald
Originated by Capstone Global Library Limited
Printed and bound in China

17 16 15 14 13
10 9 8 7 6 5 4 3 2 1

Library of Congress Cataloging-in-Publication Data
Throp, Claire.
A Journey to the center of the Earth / Claire Throp.
    pages cm.—(Fantasy field trips)
  Includes bibliographical references and index.
  ISBN 978-1-4109-6200-3 (hardback)—ISBN 978-1-4109-6205-
8 (paperback) 1. Earth—Internal structure—Juvenile literature.
2. Earth—Core—Juvenile literature. 3. Earth—Mantle—Juvenile
literature. 4. Earth—Crust—Juvenile literature. I. Title.

  QE509.T49 2014
  551.1'1—dc23   2013012670

Acknowledgments
We would like to thank the following for permission to reproduce
photographs: Alamy pp. 14 (© Thomas R. Fletcher), 20 (© GC
Minerals), 27 (© Inga Spence); Corbis pp. 13 (© KYODO/Reuters),
26 (© Rob Howard); Shutterstock pp. 4 (© Miks), 7 (© Kenneth
Keifer), 10 (© Justin Atkins), 17 (© Serg Zastavkin), 18 (©
clearviewstock), 21 (© Mopic), 22 and title page (© Lukiyanova
Natalia/frenta); Superstock pp. 5 (Boomer Jerritt/All Canada Photos),
6, 12 (dieKleinert), 9 (Robert Harding Picture Library), 8 (Ragnar
Th. Sigurdsson/age fotostock), 11 (Flirt), 15 (TAO Images), 16
(Jason Friend/Loop Images), 19 (Jim Sugar/Science Faction), 23
(Tips Images), 24, 29 (imagebroker.net), 25 (John Cancalosi/age
fotostock), 28 (Clover).

Cover photograph of the caves of Sarawak, Borneo, Malaysia,
reproduced with permission of Shutterstock (© gualtiero boffi).

Every effort has been made to contact copyright holders of
material reproduced in this book. Any omissions will be rectified in
subsequent printings if notice is given to the publisher.

All the Internet addresses (URLs) given in this book were valid at
the time of going to press. However, due to the dynamic nature of
the Internet, some addresses may have changed, or sites may have
changed or ceased to exist since publication. While the author and
publisher regret any inconvenience this may cause readers, no
responsibility for any such changes can be accepted by either the
author or the publisher.

Some words are shown in bold, **like this**.
You can find out what they mean by
looking in the glossary.

This cave is a good place to start drilling to the center of Earth.

Earth's Layers

First of all, we need to find out what to expect as we travel through Earth toward the **core**. Earth is a **globe** made up of three main layers: **crust**, **mantle**, and core.

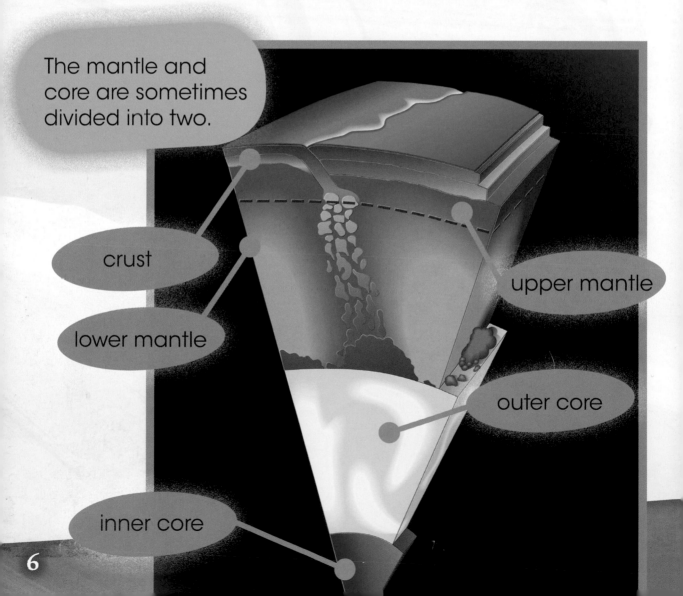

The mantle and core are sometimes divided into two.

crust

lower mantle

upper mantle

outer core

inner core

Jets of steaming water called **geysers** shoot up from inside Earth. They show how hot it is inside Earth.

The **crust** is the part of Earth we live on. The **mantle** is the next layer. The outer **core** is hot liquid, and the inner core is an extremely hot solid.

Did you know?

Cracks in Earth's crust are called **fault lines**. The Mid-Atlantic Ridge in the Atlantic Ocean is a fault line.

Earthquakes happen along cracks in Earth's crust.

Crust

Earth's **crust** is made of solid rock. The crust is thickest under mountains and thinnest under oceans.

mountains

It may be a good idea to start drilling under the ocean, where the crust is thinnest.

Earth's **crust** is broken into several large pieces of rock and lots of smaller pieces. These pieces move a few inches each year. The pieces meeting or pulling apart can change the land we live on.

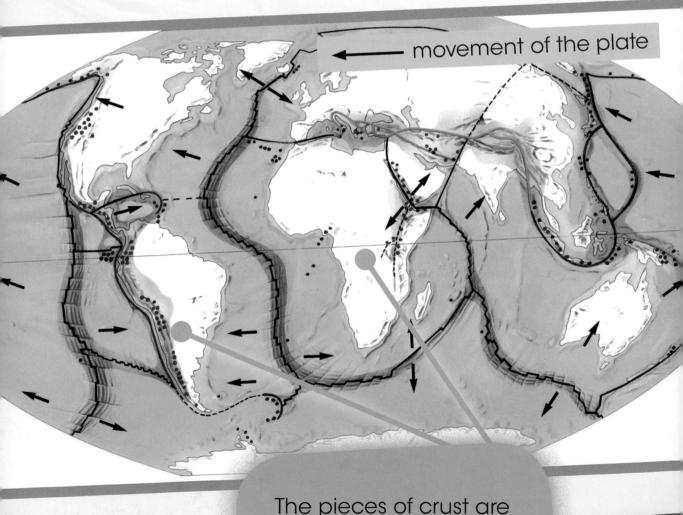

movement of the plate

The pieces of crust are called **tectonic plates**.

Drilling through
Earth's crust will
be difficult, but a
powerful drill like this
one should work.

13

Drilling Through the Crust

Deciding where to drill is difficult. Many mountains are made of **metamorphic rock**. Metamorphic rock is pushed up where pieces of Earth's **crust** meet. This rock is very hard and would not be easy to drill through.

metamorphic rock

Did you know?

The Himalayas were made from metamorphic rock that was once at the bottom of the ocean. This means it is possible to find seashells at the top of the mountains!

Most of Earth's **crust** is made up of **igneous rock**. The crust under the ocean may be thinner, but we would have to drill underwater. Let's drill through the crust under land.

This igneous rock is called dolerite.

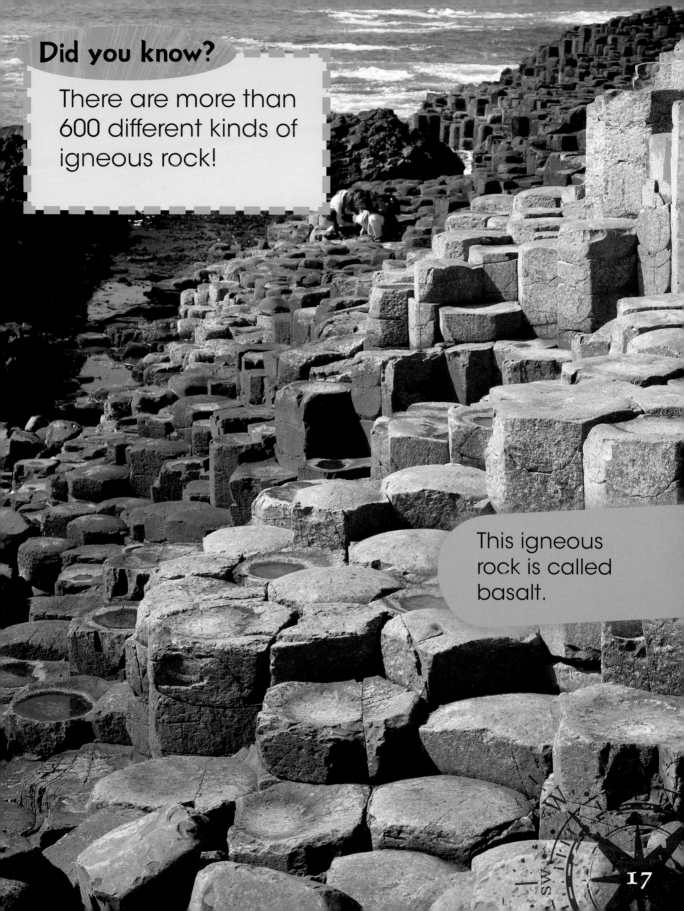

Did you know?

There are more than 600 different kinds of igneous rock!

This igneous rock is called basalt.

Upper Mantle

We have made it through the **crust** and reached the upper **mantle**. It is getting hot in here! The upper mantle is made of liquid rock. The rock is so hot that it flows very slowly, like molasses.

When hot liquid rock bursts above ground, it is called **lava**.

volcano

lava

Lava sometimes **erupts** out of volcanoes.

19

Lower Mantle

Next, we drill to the lower **mantle**. This is made of solid rock. It includes **minerals** such as perovskite. Hold on tight, we are about to enter the **core**!

perovskite

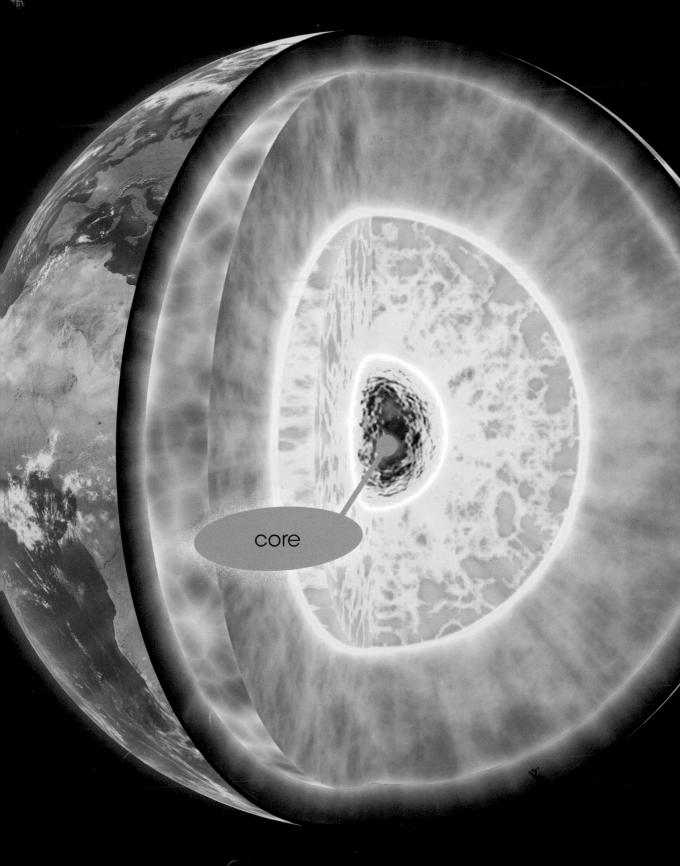

core

Outer Core

Phew, it is really hot in here now! The outer **core** is made of liquid iron and nickel. Iron and nickel are both metals. The temperature in the outer core reaches 7,000 to 9,000 degrees Fahrenheit.

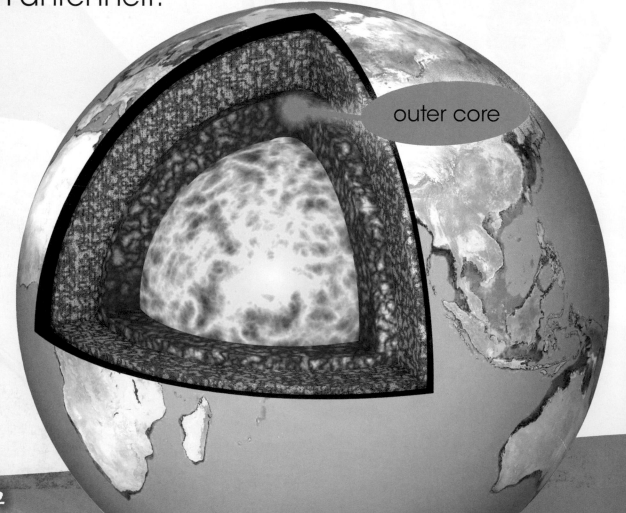

outer core

The outer core would look something like this extremely hot, melted iron.

Inner Core

We have made it to the center of Earth! The inner **core** of Earth is made mainly of the metals iron and some nickel. The temperature is thought to be between 9,000 and 12,500 degrees Fahrenheit!

You may need a towel and some water!

iron

Did you know?

The metal core does not melt because all the rock around it squeezes it into a solid metal ball.

How Do We Know?

Of course, it is not yet possible for us to really explore deep inside Earth. Scientists have discovered other ways to figure out what goes on by studying earthquakes and rocks.

This scientist is studying a rock.

This machine measures the power of an earthquake.

27

Amazing Earth

That's the end of our journey. It is time to zoom back up to Earth's **crust** and head home.

What happens deep inside Earth affects the part of Earth we see. From rocks to volcanoes, from oceans to mountains, it is all connected to what goes on way below our feet.

This is what Earth looks like from space.

Did you know?

Scientists have only managed to drill down about 7½ miles into Earth.

Glossary

core Earth's center

crust outer layer of a planet

erupt push out lava and gases from underground

fault line crack in Earth's crust

geyser jet of steaming water that shoots up from inside Earth

globe round object like a ball

igneous rock hot, melted rock

lava hot, melted rock above ground

mantle middle layer of Earth

metamorphic rock when great pressure or heat squeezes rock and changes it over time

mineral solid substance, such as gold or quartz, that can be found in the ground

tectonic plate one of a number of large pieces of rock that make up the outer surface of Earth

Find Out More

Books

Dwyer, Helen. *Volcanoes!* (Eyewitness: Disaster). New York: Marshall Cavendish Benchmark, 2010.

Landau, Elaine. *Earth* (True Book). New York: Children's Press, 2008.

Orme, David, and Helen Orme. *Inside Earth* (Become an Earth Explorer). Irvine, Calif.: QEB, 2011.

Rosenberg, Pam. *Volcano Explorers* (Landform Adventures). Chicago: Raintree, 2011.

Web sites

FactHound offers a safe, fun way to find web sites related to this book. All the sites on FactHound have been researched by our staff.

Here's all you do:
Visit **www.facthound.com**
Type in this code: 9781410962003

Index